QUIPS, QUOTES & OATS

©2010 Robert L. Merz
Revised

Previous edition copyright 2005

Published by:
Values of America Company
Haddon Township, NJ
E-mail: orders@quipman.com
Web: www.quipman.com

Cover photograph by Amber Chalfin
Book design by J. Davis Printing, Philadelphia, PA

ISBN-13: 978-0-9765868-4-5
ISBN-10: 0-9765868-4-3

Library of Congress Control Number: 2004112352

Printed in the United States of America

QUIPS, QUOTES & OATS

Smarty Jones Talks

Robert L. Merz

2010

QUIPS, QUOTES & OATS

ACKNOWLEDGEMENTS,

COPYRIGHTS,

& THE AUTHOR

***

I would like to thank my family for their great support and insights into the writing of this book. My Brother Andy, and his Wife Anne, were responsible for developing the book's title and theme. My Mother Helene, and Uncle Bill, kept me up to date on Smarty's activities and newsworthy events. My Niece and Nephews— Tracey, Geoffrey & David, made helpful suggestions in expanding this writing to the young reader. Special thanks to the Broussard Family of Claudette, Jerry, Lee, Donna, Kelly, Jennifer and Patrick for their unbridled encouragement and marketing savvy. Finally, to Auggie, the golden retriever, who teaches us all that animals have distinct personalities and spirited intellects.

***

Additionally, I would like to thank Amber Chalfin of Down the Stretch Photos for contributing the Cover photograph and interior book photos. Also, I credit Bill Herold for providing the image on page 45. All photographs copyrighted 2004. The name, image and likeness of Smarty Jones; and the distinctive blue and white silks of the Chapmans' Someday Farm are trademarks of Roy and Patricia Chapman. All rights reserved.

***

Robert L. Merz is a native Philadelphian, who grew up as a sports enthusiast and avid home town fan. He holds a Bachelor's degree in Sociology from Tulane University, and a Master's degree in Industrial Relations from The University of Oregon. He has worked for several Fortune 500 companies in the fields of sales and marketing. This is his first book. As a college student, he completed his thesis on "The Eating Habits of Horses." He has an identical twin brother who really wrote this book.

CONTENTS

***

To HELENEE'

Animal Lover Supreme

He Uses His Folly Like A Stalking Horse,
And Under The Presentation Of That He Shoots His Wit.

William Shakespeare, "As You Like It"

"They call me Smarty Jones."

CHAPTER 1

***

THEY CALL ME SMARTY JONES

***

*How the horse dominated the mind of the early races,
especially of the Mediterranean! You were a lord if you
had a horse. Far back, far back in our dark soul the
horse prances…The horse, the horse! The symbol of
surging potency and power of movement, of action, in
man.*

D.H. Lawrence

***

Welcome to my world. They call me
Smarty Jones. I am about to take you on a bit of
a ride. The opening scene is a farm in Chester
County, Pennsylvania—a hop, skip, and jump
from historic Philadelphia. It was a crisp and cool
Ash Wednesday night on February 28, 2001. The
moon was in Taurus, and Libra was rising. The
heavens were shining with shooting stars.

At nine o'clock in the evening a handsome
chestnut foal (yours truly) entered the world

"perfectly, in a hurry," according to Deborah Given, the manager at Someday Farm. My mother, I'll Get Along, was elated with her new son. My father, Elusive Quality, was overjoyed at the news and immediately handed out cigars—made of the finest imported hay.

Dad said I looked and moved a lot like his great grandfather, the legendary Secretariat. My mom knew she had something special out there on field 7. In fact, if other horses came near me, she would run at them with her ears pinned back and give them a swift kick. Now that could smart!

I was easy to spot among the other horses by the white patch on my forehead—in horse circles this marking is called a "star." Pretty soon I had lots of playmates, among them one by the name of Some Image. He could romp OK, but I used to run circles around him. Some people might call this child's play. I call it horseplay. Yes, even at a young age, I was a competitive athlete.

My owners Roy and Pat Chapman got the news and were so excited. Pat thought back to a young girl who lived in Tuscaloosa, Alabama in the 1920's. Her name was Mildred McNair. Her grandparents, Mama and Papa Jones nicknamed her Smarty Jones. That girl was Pat's mother. She was an incredible woman who liked to tell jokes, and was said to be somewhat of a smarty pants. Her birthday was the same as mine. Eureka! My name was set, and as Roy said about me, "Well, we couldn't really name him Mildred." This would be the first of many wise decisions made by them.

Roy "Chappy" Chapman and Pat met many moons ago when Roy was selling cars, and Pat was looking for a new ride. Little did they know their meeting would provide a ride of a different color, not to mention a horse of a different color. They had developed a mutual interest and love of horses, and figured the time was right to get into the business. They were always dreaming that "Someday we were going to do this, and someday we were going to do that." Well, they did it. The time was 1988, and the place was named 100 acre Someday Farm in New London, Pennsylvania. The farm was originally purchased to raise horses for fox hunting and racing. Roy and Pat were naturals. From the onset they were winners. One of their early horses, Uncle Merlin, was so good he participated in the Grand National Steeplechase Race in Liverpool, England. Boy, that's kind of a long jump across the pond from Pennsylvania to England!

I'm a red, chestnut colt of average size. They say my best features are a fine head and lustrous red coat. I've been nicknamed "Little

Red" after my ancestor Secretariat who of course was "Big Red." Although not a big horse, I have been referred to by my trainers as "A little piece of iron." In terms of size, I'm about 15 "hands" and 3 inches. A hand is an equine (that's Latin for horse) measurement of 4 inches, like the width of a human hand. So let's do the math. I'm about 63 inches as measured from the ground to the highest point of the "withers" (the ridge between the shoulder bones).

I was born with the perfect combination of athleticism and power. I weigh a little more than a half ton and can reach speeds of up to 45 miles per hour. I wear what are known as racing plates, or as you call them, horse shoes. I wear ultra-light aluminum shoes with high-tech rubber pads for my front feet, and wedged heels for my hind legs. They have "toe grabs" that give me the traction I need. I get a new set every 2-3 weeks. As they say in the horse world, "An ounce on the hoof equals a pound on the back." If this sounds like a TV commercial, it's because I want all the sneaker companies to know I'm available as a spokeshorse. I already have a name for my shoe. It's based on the athlete who comes out of nowhere to dominate the game. You got it, it's called the "Smarty Ringer ©."

My family tree, believe it or not, goes all the way back to 1791, and a horse named

Hoskins Melzar, whose owner was a gent by the name of John Hoskins. I know this because I called Jim Green, the librarian for the Library Company in Philadelphia. He told me this lineage goes back eighteen generations. I am a Thoroughbred horse—a breed from 18th century England, where English mares were bred with three imported Arabian stallions. All Thoroughbreds are descendants of Godolphin Barb, Darley Arabian, and Byerly Turk who were first brought to England between 1690 and 1730. I hope you are taking notes on all this, as there will be a quiz at the end of the book.

I have another relative you may have heard of. He was my fourth cousin on my mother's uncle's side. He lived in Germany during the early 1900's. His name was Clever Hans. This is an honest to goodness true story. Clever Hans was able to solve math problems, tell time, and identify the names of people. His owner, Wilhelm von Osten, was a retired schoolmaster, positive that the horse intellect was equal to the human.

Clever Hans communicated by tapping out the alphabet and numbers in hoof taps. He enjoyed world wide acclaim. One day a "neigh-sayer" by the name of Oskar Pfungst uncovered what he thought was Hans' secret. He did a test where he moved everyone out of the room. In this situation, Hans was unable to answer the questions. Pfungst reasoned that Hans was picking up subtle clues from others in the room, and could sense any tension, tipping off the answer.

I happen to know for a fact that Clever Hans was putting them on. He really knew the answers. I heard this through what is known as our "carrot vine." It's like your "grapevine" but it goes back to the beginning of time. Since the earliest of years, humans have studied what they call "common sense." We in horsedom call it "horse sense." What it means is that things are not always as they appear. Try reading the "Daily Racing Form" and picking the winners, and you'll know what I mean.

Since I'm speaking on behalf of the Horses of America Society, I also want to reinforce the fact that we have really incredible senses. Our sight, hearing, and smell are unusually adept. We have outstanding memories, and can learn complicated tasks, a la Clever Hans.

My most recent pedigree is filled with class, speed, power, and elegance—if I do say so myself. As I've mentioned, my great-great grandfather on my father's side was the fabled Secretariat. I am also descended from another Triple Crown winner, Count Fleet, as well as the famous Native Dancer and Nashua. Of course, my sire Elusive Quality holds the world record for the mile on turf. Other notables in my gene pool include Foolish Pleasure and Gone West. Let me tell you, talk about pressure, it ain't easy being me!

At this time, I would like to give a history lesson. Yes, you are about to get an education. Let's look back to the origins of the horse. Over 50 million years ago, the first ancestor of the horse was determined to be a 10-20 inch high animal called "Eohippus." Sounds like a seahorse to me. About 20 million years later, we had grown to two feet tall and were referred to as "Mesohippus" or "middle horse." Another 10 million years forward, we were 3½ feet tall and tagged "Merychippus." Now, that sounds like a happy horse! Finally, by the time of the Ice Age, around a million years ago, we became the modern horse known today as "Equus." This is what you call being ahead of your time.

If you look back to the earliest horse riders, scientists have said that in the ancient city of Susa in southwestern Asia, men first rode horseback over five thousand years ago. Old stone tablets from around 1400 B.C. show horses being trained by the Hittites for battle and sport. Six hundred years later, the Assyrians were known to hunt lions in chariots drawn by two horses. Yes, the horse (with a little help from the gladiator) was really the king of the jungle. Also back in these wild times, ancient artwork shows the early Persians playing a little polo.

As early as 400 B.C., the Greeks wrote about horsemanship. The Romans also became skilled riders. During the first century, Romans were hot to trot on chariot racing. The "Circus Maximus" had as many as 24 races a day, complete with bookies, tip sheets, and odds. Talk about a circus atmosphere.

In addition, you certainly know about the epic story of "The Trojan Horse," where Greek soldiers hid inside a giant wooden "gift" horse, entering the gates of Troy, and capturing the city. Do you think they could have pulled this off inside a rhinoceros or elephant?

Since these days, the horse had become the animal of choice when heading into battle. Throughout history, powerful "war horses" were bred, able to carry soldiers wearing heavy suits of armor. William the Conqueror in 1066 used knights on horseback to invade England. When armies discovered gunpowder during the 1300's, lighter steeds with blazing speed were the new heroes in combat.

If we fast forward to the early years in the development of America, it should be pointed out that the first colonists found nada horse. The American Indian discovered the horse when Spanish Conquistadors brought them to Mexico in the early 1500's. By the year 1600, Indians in the western plains were riding horses in battle and to hunt buffalo.

The importance of horses in helping to forge this great Country of ours cannot be overstated. During the Revolutionary and Civil Wars, the mounted soldier led the way. We were the force in moving the supply wagons, and hauling that beast of a weapon—the cannon. Let me tell you, the noise coming from this oversized gun could buckle the knees of even the strongest horse.

I read in one of my history books that George Washington liked to race horses, and even served as honorary steward for the Maryland Jockey Club. Horseracing as we know it in the United States, really gained appeal during the 1823 match between American Eclipse and Henry. A crowd of sixty thousand people gathered on Long Island, at the Union Course, to see American Eclipse win. To this day, horseracing folklore has given us the term "eclipse" to signify a come from behind winner.

As America expanded and exploration took off, horses pulled the trains until the steam engine took over in 1830. I believe this is where you get the expression—"to let off a little steam." We also pulled the streetcars (known as "horsecars") until you finally invented electricity. What took you so long? If you ask me, from what I've heard, there was entirely too much time spent searching for gold and carousing in those Wild West saloons.

Of course, let us not forget the Pony Express and stagecoach that delivered all your mail, till the telegraph brought the east and west together in 1861. The Pioneers, who opened up the West, couldn't have achieved this without the covered wagon. Do I have your attention now?

Naturally, the world has become a very modern place due in part to the will of the horse. Today, machine technology of steel and metal knows its roots—no wonder our railroad is called the "iron horse," and automobile the "horseless carriage."

This concludes our lecture on "How the West was won." If you're walking around town tonight, or are out for a stroll in the country, please remember that everyday is "Hug a Horse Day!"

"They call me the Philly Flyer!"

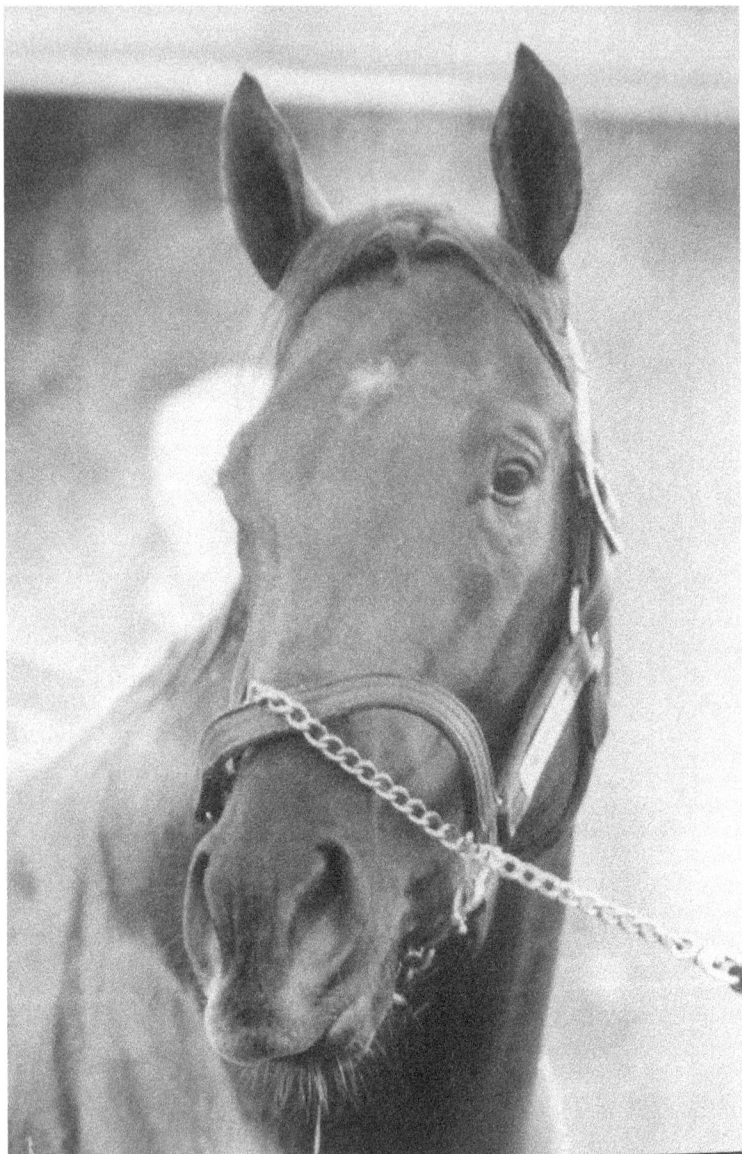

"My family treats me like 24 carrot gold."

CHAPTER 2

***

MY FAMILY

***

Over the river and through the wood,
To grandfather's house we'll go,
The horse knows the way
To carry the sleigh,
Through the white and drifted snow.

Lydia Maria Child

***

It was in 1993 that the Chapman family first got serious about Thoroughbred racing. Their trainer and advisor Bob Camac recommended they buy a yearling filly for sale at Keeneland in Kentucky. They opened up the piggy bank and came up with 40 grand for the beautiful I'll Get Along. A bargain in today's racing world, as she netted close to 300 thousand dollars in her distinguished career. Now let's move forward to the early part of the year 2000, when I'll Get Along is paired with the stallion

Elusive Quality (for a very modest 10 thousand dollars). Voila, sparks fly, and the offspring is you know who.

Roy and Pat Chapman are my guardian angels. They have been truly selfless in giving me the best, even though they have experienced intense personal setbacks. Roy suffers from emphysema and is bound to a wheel chair and breathing tube. His health made it necessary to slim down their stable of twenty horses, and relocate to another farm in 1999. When the Chapmans tragically lost their dear friend and my mentor Bob Camac in late 2001, they were thinking of getting out of the business and selling all their horses. Instead, they trimmed the operation and kept me in the fold.

I was on the auction block for a while, having been sent to Bridlewood Farm in Ocala, Florida. The general manager, George Isaacs, was to shop me around and see what the market would bear. There was an offer for 250 thousand dollars. I cringed. I saw myself prancing around at the Pier Show in Miami Beach. George told Chappy about the offer, but he also told him, "This may be the horse you've been waiting for." Chappy respected the word of George, and trusting his gut, had me shipped back home. He knew, as they say in the racing world, that I could really "turn a foot." My new home would be Philadelphia Park.

I was glad to be back in Philadelphia. I love my home at Philadelphia Park. You've heard of the "blue blood" horses and their posh pads; well I'm a "blue collar" horse who lives on the same grounds as the State Fair. I love the Ferris Wheel but of course I'm partial to the Merry-Go-Round. Philly Park is located in the citified suburb of Bensalem, bordering Northeast Philadelphia—or as we call it in Philly—The Great Northeast. Philadelphia is a great town with some of the most passionate sports fans on the planet. They have a real affection for the hard-working athlete who goes the extra mile. Roy is always talking about the Philadelphia spirit, having grown up in the established Germantown section of the city. I have been embraced by the people since day one. They call me the Philly Flash and the Philly Flyer.

Upon my arrival in Philadelphia, the Chapmans were facing some decisions. They liked to call themselves ham-and-eggers in the racing business, and were in need of a first class trainer to get Team Smarty off and running. They sought counsel from Mark Reid, a friend and former trainer, who was highly respected in the industry. Mark said there was one top guy for the job—a young man with deep roots in horse racing, who was looking for quality horses. That man was John Servis.

John brought me under his teaching, and included me in his Philly Park stable where I would be a part of Barn 11. John had a great group of people in place. His team included stable foreman Bill Foster; assistant trainer Maureen Donnelly; groom Mario Arriaga; and exercise rider Pete Van Trump. In time, my jockey Stewart Elliott would be added to the mix. And of course the one person who has been with John all along, his wife Sherry.

My career at Philly Park started out a little rocky (just like the mythical Philadelphia boxer). I was kind of raw in terms of talent when John first looked at me in mid 2003. I had been schooled on the fundamentals as a yearling during 2002 while in Florida, but I was a long way from hitting my stride and the racing circuit. As fate would have it, a month into training with John, I had a bad accident in the practice starting gate. I did a number on my noggin, smacking it into the overhead pole. That is not what I call using your head. They said I would never race again. (There will be more of the gory details later). This set back my training for several months, but with some luck, hard work, and special attention, I rebounded.

Beginning in November of 2003 I went on a run of consecutive winning races. It started at Philly Park on November 9th with a debut six-furlong race (a 7 ¾ length win), and then two weeks later, the seven-furlong Nursery Stakes (a 15 length romp). After celebrating the New Year, I hit the track on January 3, 2004 and took the Count Fleet Stakes (a mile and 70 distance) at Aqueduct in New York by 5 lengths. We then took our show on the road to Oaklawn Park in Arkansas, and on my birthday, captured the mile long Southwest Stakes by a close ¾ length margin. We continued at Oaklawn three weeks later, breezing to victory in the 1 1/16th mile Rebel Stakes by a cool 3 ¼. Staying with a three week schedule, we nailed down the Oaklawn hat trick on April 10th, claiming first prize in the 1 1/8th mile Arkansas Derby by 1 ½ lengths.

On May 1, 2004, my sweetest dreams came true. I celebrated spring with my own May Day celebration, prancing around the maypole as I won the mile-and-a-quarter Kentucky Derby at Churchill Downs. Now I know the feeling when they say hope springs eternal, and a horse's fancy turns to roses. I was on top of the world. I had attained the crown jewel of racing. My 2 ¾ length victory was a major accomplishment.

My jockey Stewart Elliott sized up my performance in our winning stretch run:

Lion Heart was sitting, but I knew I had a loaded gun underneath me. And I was just waiting. As long as nobody was coming at me from behind, I was just going to sit till he straightened up. He switched leads, and I figured it was time to go, and he went to running.

Two weeks later, I shocked the racing world by winning the 1 3/16th mile Preakness Stakes at Pimlico in Maryland by a gaudy 11 ½ lengths. Now I was really strutting my stuff. I was thinking of the famous parade they have in Philadelphia on New Year's Day. It's called the Mummers' Strut—featuring great music, colorful costumes, and slick dance moves. I felt like I had just taken first place in the fancy brigade competition! All of a sudden, I was The Man. The Horse. I sat at the doorstep of the first Triple Crown in 26 years.

The next three weeks would be the most intense ones of my young life. Without giving away all the details now, I will simply say that even the Smarty Party had to take a break. My 8 game win streak came to an end at the Belmont Stakes in New York, with a tough second place finish on the long 1½ mile oval at Belmont Park. C'est la vie. During the past five months, I had run seven pressure races against the best in the business. That is a marathon of hoofing. I couldn't be prouder of my accomplishments. I owe it all to the individuals who made me into a contender and champion.

My Team is so supportive. Stewart and John are always giving me a pat on the back, making me feel special. Everyone is always trying to keep me happy. After the Kentucky Derby win, I glanced up into the owners' box and saw Roy a little misty. It got me a bit choked up too. I guess it just hit him that his journey of hard work and strong beliefs had finally come to fruition. He's kind of an emotional guy, even though he tries to stay in control. Deborah Given, who delivered me into the world, stopped by after the Derby, and she was talking about Roy: "He comes off as a rough guy. He's really a softy at heart. He doesn't want the world to know that." Bill Foster said it best when he talked about Roy and Pat Chapman: "They give people an opportunity to prove themselves. They're very straight-up people. They look for the good in people."

My crew is so good to me. Did you know that I have my own personal 50 pound bag of carrots. I get two of these each week! After I won the Derby, I had my favorite for Sunday brunch. It was a gourmet mixture of oats, carrots, bran, and sweet feed, blended exquisitely with some molasses. A meal fit for a king. On a usual day I'll consume over ten pounds of hay and carrots, including four quarts of oats and sweet feed in the morning. During the afternoon and evening, I polish off another 10-12 quarts. Hence, the expression "Eats like a horse." Throw in 15-20 gallons of water a day, and you have one happy camper.

Think I'm pampered? I get triple the amount of straw to sleep on for my bed. I get six bales instead of the usual two. Now that's what I call living large. It doesn't end there. I have 24 hour security. You have to show special ID to get into the backstretch of the Park, and even then the night watchman may shine his flashlight on you. Who goes there? Sherlock Holmes I presume!

I usually get out of the barn at 5:30 in the morning. John gets up before 4:30 am, and he's at the barn before five. Don't forget that there are 44 other horses in the stable. In my mind we're all family. John is kind of a sensitive guy. In the morning I'll see him just walk around the shed for ten or fifteen minutes, looking for different things. He likes to say: "Horses will talk to you if you listen. You just gotta pay attention. Just watch them. They'll tell you." John knows. For example, he rested me between the Derby and Preakness. He reasoned that he was feeling the wear, so I was probably also feeling the weight. He was right on. Like father, like son.

I guess I am like the special son to John. He plays with me like he does his kids. He'll pat my neck and always make the last one a loud smack! I know it's coming. I'll give him a little nip, a little tug. I've learned much about John. He always does what's best for me.

John is a very hard worker. During our run through all the Triple Crown hype, he was dealing with the media, news conferences, interviews, and running his horses. He would be at both Philly Park and Delaware Park. It was kind of funny to see John at some of these formal news events, dressed up in his jeans and work boots. His focus is intense. He keeps saying "The horse is doing a lot better than I am." John could have taken it easier as we went into Belmont, but he kept going fast forward.

Did you know that when he first came to Philly Park about 20 years ago, he lived in a 25 foot trailer. Evidently, the sliding glass doors would freeze up in the winter, and he had to use a hair dryer to get out.

Now days, John lives a mile from the track with his real family. He has two great teenage sons, Blane, and Tyler. He spends quality time coaching the kids' youth football team. His wife Sherry even works the concession stand at the games. Would you like a Smarty hat with that Coke and fries? Sherry has been the "stable" force for Team Smarty. She has handled all the day-to-day planning and kept us super organized. It doesn't end there with the family. John has even enlisted the help of his cousin Donna.

John also has a spiritual side. He was an altar server as a boy. His aunt, Sister Catherine Marie, is a Nun, who often takes care of the family dog Cassius when John is out of town. She says John is carrying on the tradition of his grandfather, who delivered milk by horse and buggy in the Kensington section of Philly. I would love to do this, although I would prefer being the "Good Humor Horse" carting ice cream.

John carries in his pocket a Sacred Heart Medal given to him by Pat Chapman. It's for good luck and divine inspiration. On race day, the medal is placed under my saddle. After I won the Derby, in all the excitement, the Medal was temporarily misplaced. When John realized it had disappeared, he was more nervous than he had been at the start of the race. Fortunately, it was recovered by a friend, and now is always within his grasp. I have been blessed in many ways. I have even received a blessing from Father Thomas Homa of Our Lady of Fatima Church, the local Church here in Bensalem, Pennsylvania.

John is an incredibly loyal person. He will do anything to benefit the Team. He showed me his deep down commitment by bringing in Stewart Elliott as my jockey and staying with him. All the so-called racing experts were saying that once the Derby was in sight, John should have gone with another big time jockey. Horsefeathers! Stew had won the last three riding titles at Philadelphia Park, and guided me to six straight victories. He has over thirty thousand mounts in his long career, and has brought home well over thirty-three hundred winners. In recent years, Stew's winning percentage has approached 20%, and he's been in the money almost 50% of the time. John knew that Stewart was the man for the job, and there was full support from the Chapman camp. We horses have an expression— "don't change riders in the middle of the river."

Stew was most thankful, and taking it all in after the Derby win:

I'm so happy for Mr. and Mrs. Chapman and John Servis for sticking with me, and giving me this chance. It's a great thing. They could have rode anybody in the world they wanted to. They've given me this opportunity to let me prove myself... The excitement afterwards, just realizing where you are. It's just unbelievable.

Stewart was born in Toronto, Canada. He is a fifth generation horseman going back to the Scottish Highlands, whose father Dennis was a jockey and trainer. His mother is an assistant trainer. Stewart is a worldly guy, having lived his early years in Hong Kong where his father rode. Stew began riding in 1981 at what was then called Keystone Park. It is today known as Philadelphia Park. Stew has also ridden extensively at Atlantic City Racetrack in New Jersey, Suffolk Downs in Massachusetts, and Rockingham Racetrack in New Hampshire. I keep asking him when he's going to take me to Atlantic City. I'm a pretty good card player, and like to see the cards come out of the shoe.

We like to call Stew "Mr. Cool" because he's a pretty relaxed guy, who doesn't show a whole lot of emotion. He has so much experience that his natural abilities just take over. He reads the racing situation perfectly, and can calculate exactly when to make the right move. John knows this and lets him call his own shots. Speaking of shooting, John and Stew are hunting buddies. They go after the big deer and trophy game. John says Stew has a lot of patience waiting for the big game, and that he has bagged some big ones.

You've probably noticed Stewart's colors at the racetrack. My colors, or as we call them "silks," are blue and white. Stew's shirt is blue, and the sleeves are white with blue polka dots. The silks relate to my owners, the Chapmans. My colors were designed by Pat Chapman and Mark Reid. I love that color of blue, it's really bright— just like me! There is the letter "C" on the back of Stew's shirt that stands for "Chapman." To me it means "Caring."

Another important part of my group is my stable pony pal Butterscotch. His real name is "Scotch with a Twist," but that's a little much. He's 23 years old, and has been in John's barn for about 16 years. He's the president of AARH (American Association of Retired Horses). As the lead pony he's a big part of the stable. During the march to the post on race day, he's the one you see giving me a pep talk, and just helping me relax. He's my constant companion during workouts. He really has been a calming influence on me. He's helped me to settle down. We ship together in our pad on wheels to all the tracks. We are stable mates next to each other, and we play a little gin rummy after lunch. When the lights go out at night, we sometimes sneak in a basketball game of "horse." We shoot carrots into the feed tub.

My groom, Mario Arriaga is the guy who keeps me in tip top shape. He's my trustworthy comrade whether I'm going to the paddock, heading to the track, or getting ready for a bath. Mario is from Guatemala, and he has taught me a little Spanish. He likes to call me "Poppy." Mario says that the most important thing of his work is to take your time. Start early and take your time. My exercise rider Pete Van Trump talks about my relationship with Mario:

> *That horse is like his son. That horse listens to him. Somebody else might do something; he might kick them or try and bite them. Mario, it's like his child...Every horse Mario gets his hands on ends up looking like a million dollars. I mean that pony has never looked so good.*

Oh come on Pete, you know I'm totally low maintenance!

Pete has a great sense of humor. He is another one of the prominent people who keep me in line. As my exercise rider, he knows my moves better than anyone. At 170 pounds, he's a little heavy to be a jockey. Pete has been riding since he was 2 years old—just like me! He started on his family farm in Missouri, and has rode quarter horses. Believe it or not, he's also an experienced rodeo cowboy. I like to think I'm a smoother ride than some of those rodeo bulls.

Pete is known to have great hands and a superior feel for riding. He has been a key in helping me stay composed and train for the long races. He helped me feel comfortable in the white bridle you see me wearing. It's a special harness developed to keep my head down and give the rider more control. It has something called a German Martindale attached. If you look close, you'll see it's really an am/fm stereo radio with MP3 player. Yup, I like to gallop to hip hop!

I mentioned earlier that I am not the only horse under the wing of John Servis. His stable operates with about 26 people taking care of some 44 horses. The person who really makes it gel is our assistant trainer Maureen Donnelly. We have many intellectual discussions. She is a Cornell graduate, and will sometimes explain to mc about the meaning of being a champion. She has been able to maintain a level of excellence few can achieve. Even when John has been away during the grueling months, she has kept everything in tune. The winning percentage of horses in the stable is something like 28%. That is big time.

There's a guy on Team Smarty who I think the world of. His name is Bill Foster. Bill is the stable foreman, so he is always near by. As a matter of fact, he sleeps a few stalls down from me, and has been known to console me when I wake up after a bad dream. That one about bears sleeping under my straw really threw me for a loop!

There's the true blue story about how several years ago, Bill showed up at Philadelphia Park looking for work. His parents had recently passed away, and he was divorced. While he was walking around the grounds, an announcement was blaring over the intercom on the backside of the track, that a "hot-walker" was needed (to cool the horses down after workouts). John hired Bill and the rest is history. Bill and John have a great relationship. John says: "It's just reassuring knowing he's around. He's the guy I tell when there's something I don't like around the barn. Or I'll call him to get a phone number. I'll say do me a favor, remind me, and he'll remind me. Things like that." In the business world this is what they refer to as trust. At Team Smarty we like to take it to a higher level. It's what we call family. As Bill Foster says about his boss, John Servis, "I'm working for my best friend."

Someone asked Bill Foster if he thought I was aware of what I had accomplished. Bill replied: "Sure he does. They know they're smart, and I put him in the top echelon of smart." Now that is what I call a brilliant horseman!

"John, Is that the expensive body wash?"

"Mario, you can really turn a foot."

"Pete, you look great in that suit."

"The Undefeated Underdog."

CHAPTER 3

***

THE UNDERDOG

***

A 'dark' horse, which had never been thought of, and which the careless St. James had never even observed in the list, rushed past the grandstand in sweeping triumph.

Benjamin Disraeli, Earl of Beaconsfield

***

I guess people like me because I've been a fresh face and ray of hope during troubled times around the world in the 21st century. I heard that Charles Cella, the owner of Oaklawn Park racetrack in Hot Springs, Arkansas, likened me to my ancestor Secretariat. It seems that back in 1973, the Watergate scandal was in full throttle on all the front pages. When my great-great grandfather won the Triple Crown, suddenly America had a hero to turn to. I'm not looking to be superman, but if you want to throw some troubles my way, I'm happy to carry the weight.

By the way, that gentleman Charles Cella is a very nice man, and it has nothing to do with the fact he gave us a 5 million dollar "Centennial" bonus for winning the Arkansas Derby, Rebel Stakes, and Kentucky Derby. Mr. Cella put up this loot to celebrate the 100th anniversary of Oaklawn, and attract the best horses. Chappy said he didn't want to break the bank, but he would be a sport and take the five mill. This would be the single biggest payday in horseracing history.

The one thing I never really understood was the notion that my pedigree was not top of the line. I often scratch my head in disbelief of those so-called racing experts who said I was strictly a speed horse who would never get over a mile in distance. It seems my sire, Elusive Quality, and dam, I'll Get Along, were both considered to be burners.

The conventional wisdom in the business is you need to match speed with endurance. I checked the background of some of these scholars, and not a one has a degree in genetics. I guess they're now back in their labs trying to find the lost variable in the formula. I can tell you what the missing quotient is—it's called heart.

I often think back to when I first arrived at Philadelphia Park. There were doubts concerning my potential—even from my loyal stable mates and handlers. Bill noted, "He's well put together, but he's small." Pete wanted proof: "We'll he'll have to show me." Even John had second-hand knowledge: "They say at the farm he's the real deal." I clearly understood their positions. Many horses had come and gone through the barn of John Servis. There was always the hype and promise. I call it "Crying Horse."

I recall the first day John got a look at me. He was with Roy Chapman at Philadelphia Park. Roy tells the story:

First day we saw Smarty, he watched him work out. He sat down with me and said, 'Chappy, this is a nice horse. This horse could go somewhere.' And I said, John, the only thing I want to go to, if I got a horse like this—I want to go to the Derby.

I remember hearing Bill Foster say:

You know how many horses we've seen? Big horses, grand horses. And they couldn't run from here to there...Always, there's always a flame in your heart. We'd see the two-year-olds come in, and We'd say, 'Maybe this year.' And finally it happened, he came. Out of the sky.

As John summarized it, "Finally, somebody was telling the truth."

I may not have been born with a silver spoon in my mouth, but I come from some pretty good stock and upbringing. I know that the bluebloods in the racing community turned their noses up at me and my Team, even after our impressive wins at Oaklawn. What gives? Philadelphia is not Bluegrass Country. They said my owners, trainers, and jockey had never experienced the spotlight or competed with the big boys. This lack of experience and seasoning had rarely produced a champion in the past. It had been 25 years since a first time Derby trainer and jockey duo had won—the last being with Spectacular Bid. Everyone said it couldn't be done. There was one problem. No one ever told this stuff to me. I learned about this doubt hovering over my Team at the Kentucky Derby news conference after we had brought home the bacon. Needless to say I was somewhat puzzled.

Roy Chapman had been holding back his feelings and those of our whole Team in the days leading up to the Derby. Even among all the "Stew Who?" and "Smarty Who?" talk he kept his composure. John Servis was taking it all in stride, simply calling me the "Undefeated Underdog." I had a chance to be the first horse to win the Derby without a loss since Triple Crown winner Seattle Slew in 1977. At the winner's press conference, Roy opened up a bit, sending shock waves through that little town of Louisville:

To see a horse that was born on the farm that we had and look at the stall he was born in. I'm still a little nervous, but it's an incredible feeling. Just be careful what you ask me. I'm from Philadelphia, No. 1, and No. 2, I'm a car dealer, so I say things that are on my mind. I watched one handicapper who has been here for 22 years. I'm not sure he even mentioned Smarty's name to tell you the truth. Another handicapper said you know he's a good horse, but he's not really going to beat anybody. He's kind of a freak. I hope he reads the paper tomorrow and understands this freak just won this race today, pretty handily.

John Servis was more diplomatic. He spun some southern hospitality letting the locals know we were the best thing to happen to Kentucky. He knew the old guard might become upset with the Pennsylvania group crashing the party. He simply noted: "He's a Kentucky sire, you can love this horse. It's OK. It's a great story, and it's great for the business." They bought it…I think.

Chappy likes to say I'm a blue collar horse who belongs to the people of Philadelphia. I also heard that the Governor of Pennsylvania, Ed Rendell, referred to me as a champion of the people. I know he's a huge sports fan, and a keen observer. I understand he had money on me to win the Derby. No wonder he's the Governor— he's fiscally responsible! He had some interesting commentary after my win:

Sports brings us together as a community. The richest businessman in Philadelphia and the shoeshine man can talk about the Eagles, talk about the Phillies, talk about Smarty Jones, and they're on a level playing field. It's something we all have a part of it.

I still find it hard to believe that I've developed a fan club. I think it's great for the whole industry, bringing racing to a larger audience. Of course my biggest fans are my Team members. After I won the Preakness by the largest margin in the race's 130+ year history, John told me he got goose bumps. No one told me there were geese at the track. He said he was kind of in awe of Stewart and our performance—

how we had brought our best game, brought it big time, and come through for America.

Our ride to the top hasn't been an easy one. It has taken a great deal of work and perseverance. I remember back to the days I spent in training, especially following my accident in the starting gate. When I was at the farm getting in shape, I would spend many hours on the treadmill. This is the truth. At first, my personal trainers wanted me to take it easy. I would have no part of it. I didn't want to go slow. I didn't want to be told to go at a certain pace. I was my own boss. I would get that treadmill up to 12 miles per hour. One of my exercise riders, Bob Velez, says that I'm tough. He has exercised other horses including 1985 Kentucky Derby winner Spend A Buck. He told me I'm the toughest horse he ever galloped.

I've also been blessed with natural talent. I remember as a two-year-old, I made a move that woke up the old shed and the Philly horseracing community. I recall jumping up off all fours, turning sideways, and kicking at another horse. It has become my signature move. John couldn't believe it. He was asking me, "How did you do that? You're so light on your feet." George Isaacs, who taught me a few dance moves early in my career, likes to call me "Michael Jordan in a bridle, effortless and with presence."

Personally, as a Sixer's fan, I prefer "Dr. J." You are more than welcome to call me "Dr. S."

The thing I am particularly proud of is my affiliation with the people of Philadelphia. Like I've been saying, they have been my backbone, cheerleaders, and source of strength. No one can do it alone. These people have aided our entire Team and given us their "City of Winners" attitude. You hear about helping each other and creating a "win-win" situation. In Philly we have achieved this.

Philadelphia Park, for several years, had been experiencing difficult financial times, and not gotten stellar reviews from the racing community. Over the past decade, there was talk of trying to bring slot machines into the Park to increase gambling revenues. This would help to greatly upgrade the facilities, increase purses, and attract the accomplished trainers and horses. During our streak of victories, this issue suddenly came alive and moved to the front burner. On July 5, 2004, the Governor signed the Bill approving this legislation. What a great Independence Day Birthday gift.

The Gov (we are on a first name basis) pointed to Team Smarty, and how delighted he was to keep John Servis and crew happy. There had been horse whispers that other race tracks were trying to lure John's wagon train to greener pastures. I even got a special personal thank you. Talk about a fireworks of emotion!

The Chief Executive Officer of Philadelphia Park, Hal Handel, brought the whole Team Smarty experience into perspective:

> *It's like your son is at tech school sort of barely making it through. Then he is accepted at Harvard. He turns out to be a 4.0 student, and he comes home with Bill Gates' daughter on his arm. This is just surreal.*

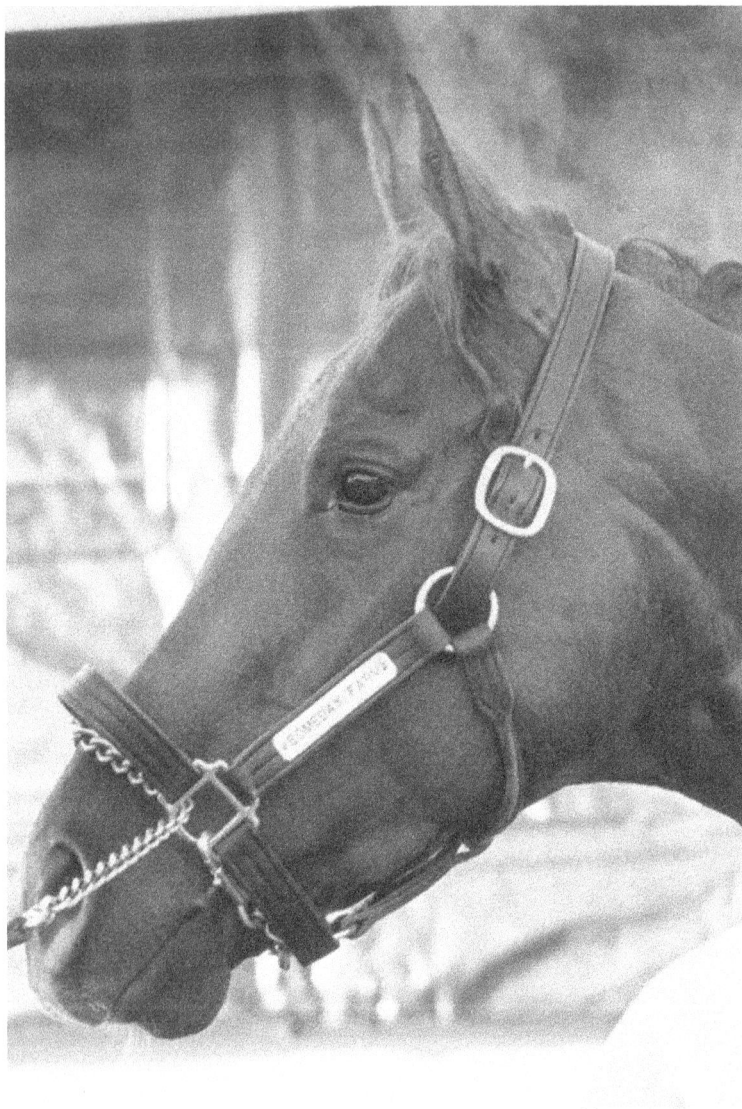

"Excuse me while I put on my game face."

CHAPTER 4

***

CONFIDENCE

***

It were not best that we should all think alike;
It is difference of opinion that makes
horse races.

Mark Twain

***

My trainer John has a pretty cool cell phone. When he turns it on there is a picture of his wife, oldest son, and his dog. His dog's name is Cassius—named after the legendary prizefighter Muhammad Ali. John likes the story of Ali, a relative unknown early in his career who shocked the world. I heard John talking to a reporter about me:

He's very cocky, and he'll let you know that he's good. He'll walk by and give you a little kick...He'll bite you. But he never does it to hurt you. He'll kick you not

hard, but just enough to let you know that
I could get you if I wanted to.

Oh come on John, you know I'm Mr. Sensitivity!

Yes, I do think Ali is great, but my main man is Philly's own famed boxer, Joe Frazier. Just call me Smokin' Smarty Jones.

You've got to believe in yourself. There is a fine line between confidence and arrogance. You've got to walk the talk. Or as we say in horse lingo, "canter the banter." John has said that I don't have a big ego. He's right; I have a huge ego—just kidding. I really don't get caught up in all the pomp and circumstance, although I do love it when they drape those flowers over me after a win, and pop the flashbulbs. My stable foreman, Bill Foster says about me: "He's a ham. He's a movie star and he knows it." That couldn't be further from the truth. By the way, who's going to play me in my life story on the big screen? Somebody call my agent and see if the great great grandson of Mr. Ed is available.

I've got goals and I know where I want to be. I have a knack of knowing when it's game time. I know when it's time to put on my game face and step up to the plate. If I've been with Butterscotch on the track a few days in a row, I can sense that a race is getting near. I'll play around a little, and let out a few squeals! At the racetrack on game day when the bridle is put on me, and they're leading me out of the paddock, I have the ability to transform myself and rise to the moment. The night before a race, Bill Foster says he knows I'm ready—my dinner is gone, my temperature is good, and my legs are cold. Do not confuse this with having "cold feet."

My schedule during the 2004 run has been rigorous. John says he knows why so few horses have won the Triple Crown. It's an incredibly tough grind for the Team and horse. Speaking for myself, I think the Team has been bearing the brunt of the load. These guys have been out on the road for a long time and put a lot of effort into me. Heck, I remember after the Preakness, I was feeling real strong—bright eyed, licking the feed tub, just checking out the whole scene.

Throughout our racing schedule, John kept saying, "We can't seem to get to the bottom of this horse." My stamina level has been off the charts. I've always been able to lay my ears back, kick out, and give a burst on demand. At the closing stretch of the Belmont Stakes, for really the first time, I ran out of gears. The mile and a half track took a little too much out of my tank, and I just fell short at the finish. I give credit to my competitors for their performance. I ran a gutsy race. It would have been nice to collect another 5 million dollars for winning the Triple

Crown, but I've got plenty of riches. There has never been an undefeated thoroughbred in the history of the sport (who retired with the Triple Crown), and after all, I'm only human!

I have also learned that the other side of being confident is being relaxed. My jockey Stewart likes to say that when I'm at my best, I'm "pushbutton." Steve Cauthen, who in 1978 rode the last Triple Crown winner, Affirmed, says I have tactical speed. He likens me to his horse—multidimensional, with the ability to settle and follow directions from my jockey. This takes training and discipline. You have to be able to focus and block out a lot of the distractions. It's what John likes to call being professional. When people tell John I'm some sort of galloping machine, he knows how hard we've worked to get to this level.

I remember in the homestretch at the Preakness, when I moved ahead of Lion Heart and cruised to an 11 ½ length victory, his trainer Patrick Biancone said I had "swallowed his horse in two jumps." Jockey Gary Stevens, who was aboard Rock Hard Ten, noted his horse had one extra gear, and I had four. In the post Preakness mayhem, onlookers were throwing the word "freak" around. My veterinarian, Bill Baker, commented: "I don't much care for that term, but I know what they mean. He's got solid conformation. He's well balanced. I've never had a problem with him, and obviously there's a lot of heart there."

I take it all in stride. To me, flattery will get you everywhere. Penny Chenery, the extremely nice woman who owned my hero Secretariat, said I was a "phenomenon." She added: "There's an exuberance about him. He's having fun. He's into it. He can do whatever he wants." What can I say?

My Team likes to think I'm a little "full of myself" at times. Moi? I'm really a very calm, cool, collected animal. I rarely show off in public. At the Kentucky Derby, during the parade to the post and after the win, there was all this screaming and hollering going on. It didn't faze me at all. I was like, let's take a little walk around the shed. Don't get me wrong, I like to stir it up at times and do a little dancin' and prancin' around the pad. I've been known to kick a feed tub or two off the wall. And of course there's my signature wheel-turn, kick-out move. Do not try this move at home without proper supervision.

I hear people saying I have charisma. They say I'm a ladies man. The girls think I'm cute. They talk about my nicely groomed long bangs. The ladies obviously go for my personality and good looks. I've had marriage proposals. I keep hearing they think I'm tall, dark, and handsome.

And rich. I fail to believe they're only after my money. It's because I'm the strong, silent type.

Everything in my life has certainly moved into the fast lane since I reached celebrity status. John says that when the flashbulbs go off, I just want to stop and pose. That I love the attention. He noted, "So many good horses are like that. When I was a kid, I think back to John Henry. He was like that." I don't really mind the press, but it was a little unnerving when I left Philadelphia Park for the Belmont Stakes in New York. I appreciated the police escort, but the three news helicopters in pursuit were a little over the top. Hey, I made a pun! Upon arriving at the Belmont, there were like 1200 reporters, from as far away as South Africa, not to mention the 120,000+ fans who attended the big race. Yes, I have been on a few magazine covers, but that's simply because of my good looks.

The thing that has kept my confidence sky high, has been the incredible support I have received. You're not going to believe this, but after I won the Kentucky Derby, the Governor issued a formal proclamation marking May 15, 2004 as "Smarty Jones Day" in the Commonwealth of Pennsylvania. I wasn't even aware that I was only the second Pennsylvania Thoroughbred in history (after Lil E. Tee in 1992) to win the Derby. Check this out:

***

WHEREAS, Smarty Jones was born on February 28, 2001, on Roy and Pat Chapman's Someday Farm in Chester County; and

WHEREAS, Smarty Jones is the offspring of Elusive Quality and I'll Get Along and named for Pat Chapman's mother Mildred 'Smarty' Jones; and

WHEREAS, this special horse made an amazing comeback after a tragic injury in the starting gate just 12 days into his training at Philadelphia Park; and

WHEREAS, Smarty Jones continued his undefeated career with a thrilling come- from-behind win in the Kentucky Derby; and

WHEREAS, Smarty Jones has captured the hearts of his hometown, his home state, and in fact, the entire nation; and

WHEREAS, Smarty Jones's incredible run has made millions of Pennsylvania's citizens more aware of the need to save the equine industry in the Commonwealth; and

WHEREAS, Smarty Jones will carry the hopes of millions of Pennsylvanians on his back as he races next Saturday at the Preakness at Pimlico, the second leg of the triple crown; and

THEREFORE, I, Edward G. Rendell, Governor of the Commonwealth of Pennsylvania join with owners Pat and Roy Chapman, trainer

John Servis, jockey Stewart Elliott, and the entire Pennsylvania equine industry in recognizing May 15, 2004 as Smarty Jones Day in the Commonwealth and encourage all of our citizens to cheer for this courageous and feisty little chestnut horse with the huge heart as he circles the track at Pimlico.

GIVEN under my hand and the Seal of the Governor, at the City of Harrisburg, this ninth day of May in the year of our Lord two thousand and four, and of the Commonwealth the two hundred and twenty-eighth.

***

It doesn't end here. After the Belmont, John was in the Pennsylvania State Capital of Harrisburg to receive a commendation for Team Smarty from the State Legislature. Governor Rendell was there, and I was told he said we were "ambassadors" for the City of Philadelphia and State of Pennsylvania. I can't tell you how good that kind of stuff makes me feel. On the day of the Belmont, June 5, 2004, the commissioners proclaimed it was "Smarty Jones Day" in Bucks County, Pennsylvania. Unbelievable, who has two days in their honor?

Topping it all is the crazy rumor I've heard about re-naming the main road around

Philadelphia Park, "Smarty Jones Boulevard." Whoa, hold on to your horses. I think this is getting to be a little much. "Smarty Jones Lane" is fine with me!

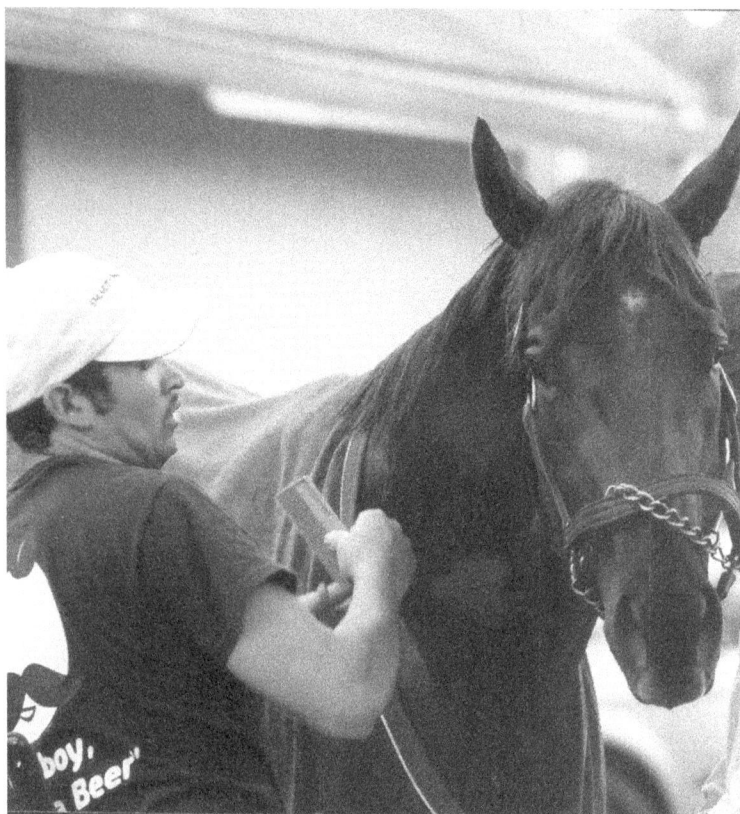

"The girls think I'm cute."

"Smarty, you are the greatest!"

"Who's the Boss?"

CHAPTER 5

***

LEADERSHIP & MOTIVATION

***

A man may well bring a horse to the water,
But he cannot make him drink without his will.

John Heywood

***

The thing I've enjoyed the most throughout my racing experience is the attention to detail and sensitivity my Team has exhibited. These guys and gals have been amazing in letting me do my thing, while at the same time giving me the right direction. I've got a little personality and my handlers know it. They know I'm my own boss with good horse sense. I have been brought along with exceptional care and training.

Early in my career, I was on the high-strung side. Like any young athlete, I had to learn to settle down and let the race come to me. My Team has taught me how to relax and focus. It has been a maturing process. I have learned that you can have all the physical ability in the world, but if you can't harness it, you lose the explosive quality. In horseracing circles it is called tactical speed.

The one individual who has really been a steadying force in my development, and perhaps the greatest leader of them all, is (drum roll please)…my best buddy Butterscotch! You've got to have friends for support and to stay grounded. I was reading about Seabiscuit, and how his whole life changed when he met up with his pal pony Pumpkin. They developed such a tight bond, that Seabiscuit became a friend to all animals—his stable mates included a dog named Pocatell and the spider monkey JoJo. And I thought I was living in a zoo!

Butterscotch is my number one companion, and he wears several hats—or as we call them "derbies." Not only is he my teacher and confidant, he's my lead pony setting the training tempo. While we are practicing on the track, he is with me (sometimes attached with a strap) until I break off and crank it into overdrive. He's there on the track to make sure I stay on course, and is my rock if anything unexpected happens. As a young gun, I would sometimes bound off the track. There was Butterscotch to the rescue.

He really earns his straw on race day during the post parade, as we walk by the grandstand and get pumped up for the upcoming competition. It can get hectic as we move through this gauntlet of onlookers. You've got to keep your concentration. He's got the experience, and I just follow his lead.

On the most basic level, my immediate leader is my jockey, Stewart Elliott. I swear this guy has a sixth sense. There is a term in the equestrian world known as "dressage." It comes from the French word "dresser," meaning "to train." It is the ability to guide a horse with virtually invisible instructions. It has become an Olympic event, and is often compared to the ballet. Yes, I will soon be appearing in "Horses on Broadway."

In the Kentucky Derby, slopping around on a messy track, Stew was unbelievable the way he maneuvered me. At the Preakness Stakes, he took me inside coming into the stretch and I found myself with nothing but daylight. I heard that Ron Turcotte, the great jockey of Secretariat, called Stew after the Preakness. Not only did he wish him luck, but he paid the ultimate compliment, calling Stewart a real professional who knows his horse, and has done a magnificent job.

A real key to my success has been the understanding between Stew and John Servis. John knows his jockey, and lets him perform to his capacity. John visualizes a picture before each race, and has an idea as to how the race may set up. He'll talk to Stew, but won't overload him with information, knowing that the race can change on a dime. He empowers Stew to ride his race. This is what Stew does best. Even in our gritty loss at the Belmont, Stew guided a great race. He had me in a position to win. We put forth our best effort. We held our heads high, taking pride in a job well done. Of course you want to win every time, but no one is perfect.

John says training horses is a "funny" business:

> *It's kind of like being in school. You keep your ears open and try to keep your mouth shut; and just learn from everything that goes on around you. Every horse is different and you just have to kind of watch and let the horse tell you. If you can do that, then you're going to be in good shape. You start trying to tell the horse what to do; it's going to be a rough road for you.*

Truer words have never been spoken.

John really has a great sense of how to manage and lead. He follows his own voice and believes in his instincts. He doesn't want to compare himself to anyone. To him, the horse business is second nature. John comes from a family embedded in horseracing. His father Joe, spent 50 years in the business, and transferred this commitment to John. I heard that when John got his first training job at Monmouth Park in New Jersey, he was living in a room at the end of the barn. He would go to the grocery store once a week to load up on peanut butter and jelly. And to think he gives me a hard time about eating oats and hay every day.

Roy Chapman says: "John is one of the best trainers, if not the best trainer to get a horse conditioned. He's very patient with the horse." Roy also recalled one of his early meetings with John, when they realized I might be ready for the big show. Chappy talked about John's preparation: "He laid me out a plan—here is what we are going to do with this horse, and if he goes the way we'll say he goes, he'll go to the Derby. He did not deviate one inch."

John is a man with a plan. Throughout our series of impressive wins and leading into the big races, all the critics from the racing community at large were out in force. They were saying John was unusual in his methods. He had taken me to Arkansas to prep for the Kentucky Derby, instead of Florida, California, and New York. He held me back from strenuous workouts between the Derby and Preakness. He brought me up to Belmont only three days before the race.

Whoa Nelly! Wait a minute. At this point in our story, we are going to pull in the reigns, kick back, and evaluate the situation. It is time for us all to play a game of "Stump the Smarty Party." I know you've been waiting for some game action. Personally, I like watching "Jeopardy" on TV, and guessing the "Daily Double." I wonder why they don't have the Trifecta. I dig the Game Channel on TV, although my favorite show is naturally Animal Planet.

OK, today's big question is: "How many horses competed in 'all' three legs of the 2004 Triple Crown?" Now let's take it even further—"How many horses competed in 'all' races of the 'Double-Triple?'" (I just made up this term—it's kind of catchy I think). That would be the 10 million dollar run of the Rebel Stakes, Arkansas Derby, Kentucky Derby, Preakness Stakes, and Belmont Stakes. The answer to both of these questions is the one and only horse near and dear to you. As a matter of fact, the last horse to win the Rebel, Arkansas, and Kentucky triple was Sunny's Halo in 1983.

Now you know why they call me the "little iron horse that could." Let's just say there was one horse that competed in this racing triathlon. I will be curious to see how many other horses try this feat in future years. I'm officially throwing out the challenge. You know what they say, "No guts, no glory."

We now return to our regularly scheduled reading. Getting back on track, all I can simply say is that John Servis has re-written the rules of training and managing. He has the unquestioned support of his owners, and a very loyal group of handlers. Here at Team Smarty we have an inner circle of mutual respect and deep trust. You can call it a collective force. My whole Team is so united on keeping me happy. They know that I like what I'm doing, and they do everything in their power to bring out my best performance. John likes to call this mental preparation. I call it the power of positive thinking.

My stable foreman, "Big Bill" Foster simply stated what I think are keys to a top notch racing program:

Number one in horse racing, you have to have the horse. Number two, you have to know what to do with the horse when you have him. A lot of people in this business have had a lot of horses, and never made it because they broke them down. It happens a lot. Mismanaged. Mistrained. All because people want to be in the

limelight. Which is where we're different.
We don't want to be in the limelight.

My goal is to make my Team happy. Whatever they want, I'm here to deliver the goods. My examining veterinarian, Bill Baker, who's been around horses for some 36 years, likes to say: "Horses are like people, in that if you're nice to them, they'll be nice to you." If you've been taking notes all along, make sure you put a big star next to that quote!

"Stew, We're going to Disneyland!

"They call me Mr. Lickety-Split."

CHAPTER 6

***

A SENSE OF HUMOR

***

I am that merry wanderer of the night.
I jest to Oberon, and make him smile
When I a fat and bean-fed horse beguile,
Neighing in likeness of a filly foal:
And sometimes lurk I in gossip's bowl,
In very likeness of a roasted crab.

William Shakespeare

***

At Team Smarty we have tons of fun. All of the people around me are always in a good mood. John Servis cracks me up. He's constantly talking to me. We like to say we are members of the mutual admiration society. The stimulating conversation is usually centered on John telling me how great I am, and how much I've changed his life. Of course, I toss back a little quid pro quo, letting him know I'm doing it all for him. It was kind of funny, but when we came back from the Preakness win, John got a standing ovation at one of the many events celebrating our victory. When he was asked about his biggest previous ovation, he quipped, "Probably when I kissed my wife at our wedding reception."

John has become quite the celebrity. I thought he looked real sharp at all the races, with his nice suit jacket on. Then I realized he was wearing the same jacket to all the races. I found out later it was superstition. I guess there's one upside to the Belmont second place finish—now I can get John a new suit coat. It will definitely be a Ralph Lauren Polo. Guffaw!

I was watching some TV one night after the Preakness (I go for sports and westerns). I saw John at the Philadelphia Flyers hockey playoff game. It was a frenzied atmosphere around him as he was signing some pictures. They zoomed in on the photo's inscription. It read: "To my favorite human." I let out a snort. John has been in demand. He said his phone was ringing off the hook. He recalled with a smile: "I was getting calls from places to do radio shows where I didn't even know they had radios." John is definitely ready for prime time.

Another interesting character is my owner Roy Chapman. I heard that after we won the Kentucky Derby, someone asked Chappy if he ever saw the storied horse Seabiscuit, who ran in the 1930's. Without missing a beat, he winked at his wife Pat and retorted, "I trained him." I'm telling you, Roy is one witty guy. The real humorist though, is Pat Chapman. She's originally from Georgia and is truly the sweetheart of the rodeo. Pat is a smarty gal having earned a Master's degree in social work from the brainy girls' school, Bryn Mawr College near Philly. There is the funny story of Pat and Roy's first meeting in 1976, when Pat bought a Ford Granada from Roy. The tale goes something like this according to Pat:

> *When I met him, he had his arm in a cast and I said, 'Oh, my, what happened to your arm?' He said, 'I was out fox hunting a couple of weeks ago and had an accident. The horse fell on me.' And I knew then that he was the most fascinating person I had ever known. I had never known anyone who had been fox hunting.*

When I think of the Chapmans, I remember a defining moment in my career. As we were leading up to racing in the Derby, my bandwagon was starting to fill up, and there were supposedly blank check offers made to Roy to sell me. Pat interjected that if her husband even thought about such an action—"They'd never ever find him." This is what I call give and take in a marriage.

I've become somewhat of a celebrity at Roy's Ford car dealership, The Chapman Auto Group. No, I am not doing commercials at this time, but I understand Cheerios may want to put me on their cereal box. Anyway, people are coming into the car dealership, asking what type of car I drive. Roy's sons, Mike and Randy, let potential buyers know you can "Be Like Smarty" and drive out in either a Mustang Convertible or Expedition. If you're taking the car down to Louisville, don't forget the mud flaps. Of course, go with all the horsepower you can get.

John likes to say my two favorite activities are eating and sleeping. Let me tell you, with all the extra attention I've been getting, my appetite has gone through the roof, and I need the afternoon siesta. One day Sherry Servis called the barn, and said a psychic wanted to come by and lay her hands on me. She probably wanted to recruit me for the traveling minstrel show. Yeah, I may be a merry wanderer, but I'm no gypsy.

I do know a thing or two about astrology. I subscribe to "Thoroughbred Thinker" magazine and am always looking for ways to get a leg up on my rivals. I really want to go to the Rodin Museum in downtown Philly, and take a look at that statue of "The Thinker." I can't seem to get my front hoof placed under my chin.

I was on the internet recently, and found my astrological birth chart. It's kind of interesting. Here's what it said about me as a being:

You are very attractive, popular, and charming. You often get your own way. You are very affectionate, but you don't like being tied down. Your patient and calm way has others looking to you for support. You can be stubborn—your attitudes were deeply planted in your youth. You are gracious and refined with others. You serve as a role model. You are helpful and understand the needs of others. You perform at your best when surrounded by positive, upbeat people. You form your closest ties with those in your immediate family. You make everyone feel at home.

You are an original thinker. You enjoy waking people up with your unique personality. You judge things fairly and are a fair critic. Your actions are dictated by strong values and morals. You like being in the action, and don't mind the spotlight, but you're not a showboat. You are restless, and find physical exercise to be very stimulating. You value your freedom and will resist attempts to limit it. You come to help those in need. You have a big picture of the world and want to benefit society as a whole. You seek the support of those close to you, to carry out your mission of helping others.

I'll tell you something—if it's on the World Wide Web it's got to be true. How do they know so much about me? They must have seen me on the late night TV talk shows. Or maybe it was one of those tabloid magazines. I was at the Farmers' Market, in the express lane, and I saw the cover story—"Smarty Says Low Carb Diet Led To Belmont Loss." Who writes this junk? Somebody call my lawyer.

When you're in the public eye, every once in a while you get the cheap shot. For me it's been 99% positive. My entire schedule has taken on new meaning since I won the Derby. My early morning workouts before the Belmont were drawing over eight-thousand people to Philadelphia Park. This was for a fifteen minute session, featuring a light breeze around the track. I was stunned. My fans are simply the best. Evidently, all the kids who showed up in the morning, thought there would be pony rides and some kind of a petting zoo. What did I tell you, I am a horse of the people.

In addition, I have found out I am a horse of the horse people. Since the Derby, my name has become a favorite for many newly registered Thoroughbreds. I read in the Jockey Club newsletter that we now have Party Jones, Sleepy Jones, Smarty Me, Like Smarty, Smarty Who, Smarty Dee, Smarty Joe and Smarty Brown.

The story of "Smarty Me" is particularly interesting. This three year old filly is a relative of mine, having been sired by my father, Elusive Quality. She originally was named Hastalavista Baby after the "Terminator" movie line. The owners, Bob and Mary Ellen Mckee decided to say goodbye to that name. Mary Ellen's nickname was "Me." There you have it. In her debut performance, Smarty Me paraded to an impressive 8 ¼ length victory. Like I said, it's easy being me!

The Jockey Club's vice-president of corporate communications, Bob Curran said: "We often see this happen with major news events or icons of popular culture." Wow, I am completely humbled. When is my comic book coming out?

My fan club keeps growing. I get bags of mail. John in jealous because most of it is addressed to me. I answer all my mail. We have nice thank-you cards. Most of the requests are for hoof prints. Would you like a 5x7 or 8x10 size? The mail comes in from all over the place. One of my favorites was from a first grader. He had drawn a picture of me in that beautiful stick figure way. All around the picture were drawn dollar signs. It said: "Smarty Jones, you're making so much money, send me some money." I told him he could be on my new reality TV show where I will be giving away 24-carrot jewelry. Imagine that. What a chunk of change!

I heard that when I was racing in the Kentucky Derby, my hometown fans were at Philadelphia Park and had the place packed. All the boxes were filled. Mark Reid Jr., the son of our Team's trusted advisor, told me later, "It seemed like every other person in line to cash their winning tickets was filling out an IRS form for extra large payouts." Of course, everyone had bet on me. I have a list of all those people, and I will be forwarding it to the young first grade boy.

Sometimes I think back on how far we've come. It seems like yesterday that I first set hoof on Philadelphia Park. Mark McDermott, who is with the Pennsylvania Horse Breeders Association, recalls my first experience:

There was this squirrel that owned the paddock at Philly Park. He'd walk right up to the horses, and people would feed him. When Smarty walked in the paddock, the squirrel came over to check him out, like 'You're on my turf now.' Smarty jumped straight up in the air, with all four legs off the ground at the same time, turned his body in mid air, and lashed out with his hind legs. No one has seen that squirrel since.

Oh yeah, "We're Jonesin" now!

"I hereby crown you Sir Smarty!"

CHAPTER 7

***

COUNT YOUR BLESSINGS

***

Never look a gift horse in the mouth.

St. Jerome

***

Let me tell you, I'm thankful for all the good things that have happened to me in my life. I told you earlier of my accident in the starting gate as a two-year-old. Now I know why they call it the "terrible two's." We were having our first practice session in the gate, and I didn't like the feeling of being hemmed in there. I wanted out. Being a pesky youngster, I leapt before I looked, and ended up knocking my bean on the upper bar inside the gate. I went down. I was seeing stars. It was a total mess. I'd rather not give you all the details, as you may be eating dinner while you're reading this. It was panic city.

Before I knew it, my crew had me on the way to the hospital. A call had been placed to the

New Jersey Equine Clinic. They were told an emergency was on the way, and it was serious—possible critical head wound, loss of an eye, severe injury. My future as a racehorse was not an issue. The question was would I be leading a normal life.

Upon entering the clinic, I was put under the care of veterinary surgeon Dr. Patricia Hogan. Her initial diagnosis was that there were several fractures around the orbital bone of the eye. My distorted eye was out of the socket, and there was a lot of swelling. It was a bloody mess.

After examining the x-rays, it was determined, by some sort of amazing grace, that I would not require major surgery. I had escaped serious injury, and had a good chance of recovery. Any thoughts of me racing were certainly out of the question—that would be putting the cart before the horse.

My assistant trainer Maureen Donnelly said I looked like something out of a horror show. Dr. Hogan and the staff at the clinic had nicknamed me "Quasimodo." I'm sure you remember this character from "The Hunchback of Notre Dame" as the child born with the deformed face, who eventually rises up to save the day. He was known for his big heart. Any similarities in this story to people or horses in real life are purely coincidental.

I stayed at the New Jersey Equine Center for about a week, and then went to a farm in Harleysville, Pennsylvania for three weeks of R&R. I had this funky bandage wrapped like a figure eight over my eye. While at the farm, Kathy Bradford was in charge of my recuperation. She was very careful with me. There was one problem—I didn't want to take it easy. As I mentioned before, I was ready to move forward and get on with my life. I worked hard to strengthen my body, and would play some chess with the others at the farm after dinner to keep mentally sharp. With excellent care, and no horsing around, I soon found myself back home. Three months later I would win my first race at Philadelphia Park.

I heard Dr. Hogan was in California during my Kentucky Derby race, watching me on TV. She emotionally said it was amazing I had won it all. She even said I looked "beautiful." (I am now blushing). Patty, I couldn't have done it without you. My family and Team keep telling me I have been a gift for them. What can I say? All I can do is try to keep them happy after all they've done for me.

I've been told I have been able to touch people's lives. John said he thought this whole experience was going to be like a sporting event, but instead it's been more like "Thank You."

John's wife Sherry told me, "I feel like this is a fairy tale and I'm in it." She recalled waking up the morning after the Derby win and saying, "Was I dreaming or did we win the Kentucky Derby." John added, "I've been trying to think of a word for all this, and I just can't. I hope the word I'm looking for is destiny. That's what I hope." Whoa, this is starting to get a little heavy.

I recall one afternoon, Sherry Servis was over at the stable, and she started telling me about her husband's dedication to the racing business. She was telling me that about five years ago, John was starting to question all the long hours. She said, "He actually asked God for guidance, give him a sign, something, a sign that he should continue to do this. And he did. He got his sign."

The Servis family is very special to me. John and Sherry are high school sweethearts from West Virginia, and have been married for 23 years. Their two sons, Blane and Tyler are my biggest fans. John says his happiest moments are spent with his kids, especially coaching them in youth football. John is the defensive coordinator for the Bucks County Bears football team. He says this is his stress releaser. To tell you the truth, I think it's easier to coach horses than bears.

John grew up a mile from Charles Town Racetrack in the Shenandoah hills of West Virginia. His father Joe was a jockey there, as well as manager of the Jockeys' Guild for 11 years, and State Steward for 18 years. His Uncle Jack was a long time Philadelphia Park jockey agent.

John was opening up one day:

I've always loved horses. At first I thought it would be fun to be a jockey, but I started to get too big. I was never afraid of horses. I would go right up to them, and I remember when I was young, I would watch every major race on TV. Then I thought training would be a cool way to go.

As a youth, John got a job working at O'Sullivan Farm—mucking stalls, foaling babies, and helping with the mares—all for $40 a week. There's a great story about John's early horse career. After high school, he bought a horse for $1000 from a New Jersey owner. He agreed to pay the owner another $1500 after its first win. The horse was named Two Fisted. Guess what? The horse won its first two races. Talk about a calling!

John continued his career working in Maryland and Florida. In 1977 at Gulfstream Park in Florida, he got a job working for hall-of-fame trainer Flint (Scotty) Schulhofer as a groom and hot-walker. In the early 1980's, as a jockey agent, he found his way to Philadelphia Park, where he joined Mark Reid as an assistant trainer. He got his training license in 1984, and let us all say, the rest is history.

During the past 20+ years at Philadelphia Park, John has been winning under the radar. He has collected some 900 wins, and had a nice three-year-old filly by the name of Jostle that won the Coaching Club American Oaks at Belmont, and the Alabama at New York's Saratoga in the year 2000. Yes, there was life (sigh) before Smarty.

John has always stayed the course with his goals. He must have known that one day all his hard work and determination would pay off. After our win in Louisville, he did confess, "I dreamed about winning the Derby many times, but I never really thought it would happen." Even John's celebrated teacher Scotty had to bow to the student: "He's a darn good little horseman and I don't know how he could have done any better."

Joe Servis stopped by the paddock one day, and he was talking about his son: "Two things stand out. The one word I see people use about John is calm. That's the key word. And when people say Thank You, he says 'No, Thank You.'" Again, like father, like son. I overheard about the first meeting of Joe and his wife Dolores (we share the same birthday) with Roy and Pat Chapman. Roy rose out of his wheelchair, embraced Joe and said, "You raised one heck of a son."

Sherry echoed these sentiments saying her husband deserves the star treatment: "He's such a good man. He worked so hard. And he sacrificed so much, but never his family, never the people he loves, more of himself. He was so selfless. There's a reason. Now, we know why."

John's brother Jason, an accomplished trainer in his own right, called me one night from his stable at Monmouth Park in New Jersey. He was talking about his brother, and how John had honored every interview request during our run for the Crown. Jason said, "That is the Servis in him. We were raised to treat people the right way. That is John, an honest, hard-working guy. He really is ice cream and apple pie."

My family and the blessings they have bestowed upon me run deep. It was way back in 1981 at Atlantic City Racetrack, that John started a friendship with my jockey Stewart Elliott. You know, you hear this word chemistry being thrown around a lot. When it comes to my Team, we have the perfect blend. The trust is there. I was told that several years ago, when Pete Van Trump broke his foot in two places, John took him to the hospital and paid the bill. Loyalty is our brand mark.

My family has charted my future in a most thoughtful way. Few people knew that I had a slight bruise on my right front hoof after our run through Arkansas, and before the Kentucky Derby. It was well treated, and I went onward without any pain. However, after the long race at Belmont, and upon arriving back at Philadelphia Park, I was starting to feel the effects of our tough grind. Remember, I had been racing continuously since November of 2003.

My Team rested me for several weeks after the run at the Triple Crown. The plan was to get me ready for the Pennsylvania Derby on Labor Day, and then the Breeders' Cup in Texas at the end of October. John knew something was not quite right when we started back to the track for workouts. I was on the tender side, and had a slight bruise on my left front hoof. Always thinking about my health and safety, my Team of handlers thought it would be best to get me checked out for any possible injuries. I was sent to the clinic, and my legs were given a high-tech nuclear scan. No, they do not now light up in the dark! Anyway, the results came back, and the news was startling—I had developed what they call in horse doctor lingo, "chronic bruising of the cannon bone in all four fetlock (ankle) joints." I'm telling you, that cannon bone injury must go back to our Civil War days of towing that giant gun.

Although not a major injury and fairly common to racehorses, this condition requires several months to heal, and there is no guarantee of a complete recovery to racing form. I would therefore be forced to miss the fall racing schedule. My next race would have to be as a four year old in 2005. My breeding rights had already been sold for a large sum of dough and oats, so the question of my future racing was up in the air. After a lot of thought and soul searching, it was decided that I would have to retire from competitive horseracing. Ouch, now that really hurt! (Further tests a few months later confirmed my Team's decision—an ultrasound exam showed cartilage erosion in my left front ankle).

To my Team, this was bittersweet news. John was a little shook up:

It hurts me. He could do things so effortlessly. He might have been the best of all time, and unfortunately he isn't going to be able to show that. I know he's a great horse. He is an exceptional individual. It hurts, but you just have to move on…I think the move he made in the Preakness was just a preview of things to come. He has responded to every challenge in his life with enthusiasm, talent, and every fiber of his being. I think he'll make a great stallion.

Roy echoed, "We are deeply disappointed for his fans, but we owe it to Smarty to do what is in his best interest." Pat added, "After all he's done, I couldn't live with myself if I thought we were putting him in harm's way. He doesn't owe us anything, and we owe him a lot."

Bill Foster, who has given his all for me, was a bit choked up: "There will never be another Smarty Jones. He is such a special horse with a great heart. Wherever he goes, he's going to take a part of my heart. I'm heartbroken."

At this point, I just want to come out and say it—I Love You All!! Please come and visit me at my new home. I am moving to the Three Chimneys Farm in Midway, Kentucky, located outside of Lexington. You know, the other day I was thinking back to our Derby victory, and the celebration afterward. Pat, Roy, John, Sherry and family were attending the annual bash in the

Triple Crown ballroom on the fifth floor of Churchill Downs' Jockey Club Suites. It was the "Out to Pasture Party," and the theme was "Ain't Misbehavin." You adults are so well behaved. Rest assured that I will be a perfect gentleman. By the way, I heard there is no curfew at Three Chimneys!

I will be residing in the former pad of the legendary Seattle Slew (who went to horsey heaven in 2002). Slew is the only undefeated Triple Crown winner in history, so this is quite an honor. My roommates on the farm will include Point Given (the 2001 Horse of the Year, as well as Preakness and Belmont winner); Silver Charm (the 1997 Kentucky Derby and Preakness winner); and War Chant (the 2000 Breeders' Cup Mile victor).

Three Chimneys' motto is "The Idea is Excellence." They have a philosophy of giving personal attention and promotion to their stallions. Owned by Mr. and Mrs. Robert Clay, this Farm began with a dream and plan on 100 acres in 1972. Today, it has 1700 acres, 130 employees, and 7 divisions. The Farm stood only nine stallions during the 2004 breeding season. Dan Rosenberg, President of Three Chimneys says, "The individual attention is the key to the whole thing. The horses are individuals. They have distinct personalities. They have needs that are constantly changing."

Now this sounds like my kind of place. I do have one concern though. How is Santa going to get the job done with three chimneys to handle on Christmas Eve? I am already putting together my wish list. I think I've been a pretty good boy this year. I would like one of those "Seabiscuit Fit Fun Toasted Oat Machines," and two pairs of Shrek thermal leg warmers.

Pat and Roy really liked Three Chimneys because the Farm is open to the public and very fan friendly. I've heard they expect over ten thousand people a year to visit. I can hear it now—"Sir Smarty will see you now!" Don't worry; I will never forget my Philly roots, and all of you who made the Smarty Party the longest running carnival of all time. I can now see the meaning in being born the day after Mardi Gras. Every great party, at some time must wind down.

I've said it before, but from the top down, there is a friendship and camaraderie within my Team that I feel is unparalleled in racing. Words that keep cropping up are humility and honor. The Chapman family has stayed the course in giving me the best of everything. Their involvement and commitment to the business of horses has set a new standard. George Isaacs, the well-respected horseman of Bridlewood Farm in Florida, put it into proper perspective:

One thing that impresses me the most is the pride of the Chapmans. They really impress upon the fact that they appreciate this horse. They feel a responsibility to the racing public and realize he has quickly become America's horse. They don't want to cheat the racing public.

I was talking earlier about all the mail we get, and how it really inspires and motivates our whole Team. There was a particularly heartfelt letter I had received. An eight year old girl from Arizona named Krista LeVick had written to me about her vision problems. She had been through multiple eye surgeries. She wears an eye patch. Her mother Gail said Krista wasn't frightened of the operations because I had come through my own eye surgery. Krista had sent me a letter of encouragement after the Belmont, and a picture of her horse Buck Shot. She said I was a role model. Wow, I am deeply touched. Roy and Pat responded for me, sending autographed pictures. They have become close pen pals with Krista.

Another letter also arrived on my touch-screen PC. It was from an eleven year old boy in Florida. His name is Beach Cutler. He was born with a rare skeletal muscle condition that has him confined to a wheelchair, breathing ventilator, and food tube. Beach wrote:

I watched you win the Kentucky Derby and the Preakness, and I think you will win the Belmont too! I'm so excited! You have inspired me to run like a racehorse when I'm walking with my physical therapist, Trent, and when I walk in the pool with my mom, my nurse times me when I'm pretending to race. I even whiney like a horse. You've lifted my spirits, and even though I breathe with a ventilator, I feel as lucky as you. The next time you get your horseshoes changed, perhaps you could save one for me. That would be GREAT! And please let your owner, Mr. Chapman, know that we are also cheering for him to be in the best of health. I hope that you know how much your incredible horse spirit has done for everyone.

John called Beach and sent him a whole bunch of autographed stuff from the Derby, and some money for his birthday. His mother, Sue Ellen, said it best talking about my trainer: "John has been an exceptionally compassionate and warm human being. When he did call, his voice was just as nice as he looks in his pictures. He's a person with an incredible heart."

The fact that people's lives have been changed for the better by being a part of Team Smarty is really beyond words. My stable foreman, Bill Foster, told me he hadn't seen some of his family members for eighteen years. He said his family had questioned him many years ago about going into the horse business. They felt his talents were best served elsewhere. Well, at Belmont Park, his family members were front and center, beaming with admiration at the job Bill has done.

This is what my story is all about. Throughout this amazing run, I've found out that destiny is really the ability to believe in yourself and strive to do your best, while learning from and giving to those around you. If you can do this, you're in for the ride of your life. Thanks for coming along on mine.

www.ingramcontent.com/pod-product-compliance
Lightning Source LLC
Chambersburg PA
CBHW051636050426
42443CB00024B/224